Floundering in a Sandbox

AF624697

Clair Watson

BookLeaf Publishing

Floundering in a Sandbox © 2023 Clair Watson

All rights reserved.

No part of this publication may be reproduced, stored in a retrieval system, or transmitted, in any form or by any means, electronic, mechanical, photocopying, recording or otherwise, without the prior written permission of the presenters.

Clair Watson asserts the moral right to be identified as author of this work.

Presentation by *BookLeaf Publishing*

Web: www.bookleafpub.com

E-mail: info@bookleafpub.com

ISBN: 9789357216807

First edition 2023

DEDICATION

To whomever is a fish in a sandbox.

and my dearest mother.

Blank Page

So many opportunities for ruin
Wrong choices of letters, words
Then thoughts spiraling just like this year
Twirling like shit
Even as twinkle lights and overworked inflatables
Decorate the yards as pumpkins sink in on themselves
Readied for their god on the steps of other bougie houses
Feeling like that last forgotten skeleton hanging by the gutter
Out of time by some misstep of the neurons
Nocturnal hours make the passing of the sun into
Nothing but a myth when all I see is a reflection of what was
Surrounded by speckles of multitudes

In the dark I hope the raccoons find feasts
As I clutch my earl grey the sky's so much lighter
Then my own flesh and I bet its word choices
Would be too ancient to ever know
For it chuckles at horoscopes and us wishing on
Long dead balls of gas

But the paradoxical half glass of water says
Also opportunities for the better
A good flow, a story, something akin to a plot
Or a rhythm of alliterations

To comfort the calamity of constant contusions
From unavoidable reality
A steady clackity clack of keys and ice from
One of two drinks
Faux control over the loss of job, bruises on ribs
My sick cat finding ever new places to release her bowels
But my accomplice is here.
A door away. A simple knock and request
And that alone lets me look and nod
that yes
half full the glass may be

Relived

Boy, could I use nap
Tiled memories haunting
Nothing I can do

Better Places to Be

At the bottom of the well
Yeeting back wishes
Collecting the better ones

Crossing diagonal against traffic lights
Hearing the cacophony of horns and blasphemy

Haunting graveyards with harpsicord music of popular tunes
Eating picnics with the angel statutes
Before erecting a Baphomet
Near the houses of those that protest
Planned Parenthood

Luxuriating on a tree branch on a popular path
invisible
whispering odd platitudes from the ferns
I wish I knew the end of the path before the incident
Sometimes bad things happen out in nature
especially when I've laid the trap

Stacking books in college libraries
So cryptic prophecies can be
Extrapolated from their spines

Eating a Bavarian pretzel with
Mustard and beer cheese
Chuckling with a glass of

Some random cocktail mix
That tasted of nonexistent fruits

Nothing feels more wrong then me
Floundering in a sandbox
Of flopping on the sands
Only graced with rain
When I should I have been

Chaos

Watching others flip floppin'
About in children's sand
As I munch on chips and sip
Green tea wine with a straw
So many better places to be then
This mortal flesh

Over a Year

I don't even fully remember the last time I saw Grandma
It was in a stranger's house their first floor hospice care
Can never really return home from work that way
Her memory even worse
My orange owl painting on the wall
courtesy of my sister.
I held her hand as she complimented my hair
And my bright shirt. Familiar words. Comfort
She deserved better sons
Better treatment
At some point her wishes
Were hazardous and no one would listen
And now over a year later
You're not in the ground.
You would have been a century old
And still no funeral and no word of one
Some day when the seasons warm
I'll grab a tea and put out some seeds
And watch the birds and think of her
A one person memorial service

Liminal Gothic

Is it easier to jump into the abyss
Or toward the ground?
One is a known promised pain
The other a dip into what is every latent fear

Unknown

The ground could also get you there too

The grotesque says nothing
The gargoyle vomits out the rain
The evening is still, wet, chill

Am I protected better from evil or god on a gothic church?
Your mugs should keep away the evil
But these weaponized roofs look blasphemous
The hubris of changing your feet to tower one hall
Of worship over another, buttressed
Yet the ceilings keeps collapsing
Never complete

Patting the cold granite illicit only
Spine chills and silence.
Cars honk below a din subdued by weather
Rain drenches all

Less unknown. Would knowing everything
Create more fear or lessen it?

Laughter filled the air.

The statues don't know
I don't know. We won’t know.
The universe expands
and then more unknown

Merchandise

For years, maybe decades
I have been struck with the problem
of what if I get isekai'd and in that world
I am in that merch.
Will this happen?

No.

Does this problem plague my mind?

Yes.

How do I hide the shirt? The keychain?
Why do I have a whole outfit dedicated to this crazed villain?
And a hat? With added pins?
How do I hide the fact I am enamored with evil?
The guy who burned down a village and evil speeched about how humanity is dirt and needed a tyrant
How do I quickly ditch incriminating attire before
I am drawn and quartered?

No clue.

Will I stop this past time?

Can't.

Who I Want To Be

I will never become who I want to be
not for lack of hard work or lack of time.
Nothing so easy to blame.
It's not about how many more seconds I have,
how much dedication, tenacity I have floating
in the mitochondria that composes me.
Its an impossible task cuz the point keeps changing with time:
-I want to be outdoorsy
-I want to be more impulsive
-Want to be less controlled by anxiety
-I want my medication
-- to drain away
    the excessive spiraling thoughts
    the useless hateful not me

It is an ever expanding idea.
I may never fully reach it.
I will never fully reach but as long as I grasp out
trying to over extend my arm to know
then
I am going the right way

Mushroom Circle

It is time to hike
Up into the woods
Become lost amongst the ferns
Beyond the light pollution
Out where cryptids are seen
Not camping
Laying on lumpy earth
Under the scrutinizing stars
It's for smashing pots
And screeching and wishing
stumbles into prayer
For the fae to come take me away
So many stories of being spirited away
Of vanishing into the ether
They could take another
What's giving my name
When all my information
Is already tethered and spread
About an invisible web
How worse could faeries be?

Systematic Forced Prophecy

The dominoes are laid out
one by one by one
in swirls and curls
covering the floor
any stumble or ill placed thought
could create screams and tears
more tedious work
if not a whole redo
yet with one single tap
the right flick
the destruction is wanted
the destruction beautiful
the organized chaos
has fallen in your image
and the stars weren't even aligned
yet the forced prophecy is satisfied
you are a hero

Another Day

More humdrum end of the world
The calamities have arrived
Fire, fire, everywhere but not a place to rest
Just another sip of cream soda
As echoes of others fill the air
What number was this again?
Two? Five? Hundred?
So mundane now
From up on the hill the alarm is evident
Panic real in the frenzy of those
So very far and below me
My beverage is cold and the ice clinks
It's so hard to feel sympathy
When I have felt that for so many
Years at a distance
The hill isn't immune
The hill will be breached
Has been, is, and will again
But the end of the world is nothing
Hard to fear what I've survived
So many times before.

Aquarium

Something about aquatic life
Trapped behind thick glass
On land is soothing to my soul
Their lives controlled to the
saturation of oxygen and salt
The octopus pressed against the curved glass
The jellies floating in infinity
A hidden eel amongst the coral
An adequate fake world

The Dream

I want to twirl through worlds

See pigeons croon on stages
Cooing out lines of violence

See a day pass in an hour
Sunrise and sunset

See sorcerers cast spells in
Colors my eyes will never hold

See old gods at brunch
and start salacious rumors

See fish in the sky, birds in the water
And myself happy

Saunter and roll
Until something
feels like home

A Break

I want some silence
For a reason I hate
My chosen events
Have been a din
With no conductor
And no musician
Wrote any note
A quiet room
A quiet time
It shouldn't be this
Hard to achieve nothing

Holidays

Ever since the magic of innocence
Faded with age and reality
Deaths of grandparents
They just don't feel the same
The cozy house in the woods
The smell of stuffing
The fights over it
The frozen sourdough waffles
Gathering with games
And tradition that no longer can apply
Seeing cousins
I miss the joy
Actual free time to relax
Being an adult is nothing but money
And not having any
Crying and staring at how icy the
Sidewalks and roads are gaging
Life verses nature for a few bucks
Is it worth danger ?
And every year?
    no
No it isn't

Sleepless

Hour is late
And though I was up early
My brain is active in the worst
Possible ways
Faux conversations with parents
With cousins, with people I haven't
Even seen since high school
People I don't even want to see
People who hurt me
Who changed at a crush
Who judged my cheap
Frozen meals and implied
I hated my intestines
Federal minimal wage
Gave me no choice but hatred
My body wants rest and I want rest
My brain broke and or burned the curtains
They wont come down and the show is forced on
Even as I snuggle up under my blankets
Hugging my fox plush named for a dead author
Trying to shut out what's inside me
But the hour is becoming early

Note

I wrote this
On paper and it
Will go back to
Being on paper.
Suspended in fiber
Optics under oceans
Somewhere else
I will never see
In something
Physical, man made
Wonder that we
Just keep making
worse and that
is just how we are
We war. We kill.
We try to be nice
Even w/o anonymity
We say such horrid
Things promising
Tortures only humans
Could have thought of
And I don't even think we're
Born evil but we're born
Selfish and idk what to do
about that

Aged Book

I have a book copyrighted in 1883
A guide to the Northern Pacific Railroad
It was two bucks. A gift
A hole adorns its spine
Its binding squishy its knowledge outdated
Pages so delicate I fear the oil from my fingers
Each time I want to peruse the contents
But trains have fascinated me for a long time
The sound of rails. The classic choo choo
The first train accident was an explosion
On a mountain if memory serves me
The valve got stuck and kaboom
But no fatalities and I think about this
And the rails a constant steady path
Sure you can deviate but only if triggered by
An outside hand by careful planning
The scenery changes with time with season with perspective
The sounds change with construction with efficacy
Even from the apartment I hear them from down the hill
The shrill warning that it is moving that the train could kill
And that sound soothes something in me
That I could never put down into a coherent phrase let
Alone a sentence and the last time I was on one that wasn't the
Seattle light rail I was too excited to read or sleep or really write
And I was so upset that the woman in the window seat slept
I wanted that seat. I wanted to watch as Virginia, North Carolina
And South Carolina zoom. My brain repeated I'm on a train

I’m on a train I’m on a train I’m on a train
And the euphoria of it was worth the 90 something ticket price
I could I have gotten there cheaper by air but looking down
On the ground where the world is but a too big quilt
So different then watching the houses and people and
The little slices of life you can see from a train window
Gives me short stories then the omniscient
Over view that seems so unreal from a plane
Where it feels closer to death in the sky, over oceans, and mountains
But over feels less powerful then through
Through a mountain takes so much more dynamite

Promise

My younger self would be so proud
and amazed I am alive
after all that pain and 2 surgeries

Even in Italy I would paint boxes into
oceans for my stuffed fish,
Cappuccino, ribbon leashed for puppetry

Of little charity bought gift tags
at the cash register of an American diner
2 packs made 1 mini booklet of poems
matching the Christmas image on its
opposite page as I munched breakfast
foods at night

Always holding a pencil or a pen or both
crashing a moped because I refused
to set down, pocket, or take the mechanical
writing tool from my fingers
ended with me on a recliner with a bag of frozen
peas and a scraped up shin. I remember the gnome
on that pile of wood that ruined me

For all the notebooks set on my desk
covered in cutout comic stripes
in 50 cent stickers from places that
no longer exist. So worn and duct taped
that it's hard to tell its spine is spiraled

the graphite from ages ago smudged
every page.

Just being known as a writer in the family
going to Evergreen for English
just wanting to read and write
and write and read with no math bullshit
of accidentally finding myself qualified for
MFA program and graduating

There is no way I will want to break this
ever growing, ever staying promise
of being a writer and one day
you will hold more then just this book
with my name emblazoned across the cover

I promise.

Past Presents

The amount of poems I have to write dwindles
as do the days of this year and I can't wait
for this year to be nothing but old planners
and memories. To be nothing but another
mental burden to add into the Santa sized
sack I haul. Sometimes I can put it down while
I ride a rollercoaster for a brief respite as I have
a shared meal with my sister, my mother, a friend,
my accomplice. But it is always there. I know its weight.
It has sadly become a comfort. A consistent item that
will always be with me full of sixth and seventh grade,
car accidents, the breakdowns, of cashiering and assholes,
being laid off for bullshit reasons right before
Thanksgiving.
With time the bag gets lighter.
The bag forgets what it holds.
I forget what it holds.
Some days it's almost both.
Some days it's too much.
But my grave will come no sooner then it is written
in some prophecy of stars or tea leaves in a vague
Cassandra post online. I will take it with me
and share it slowly. Hard to be overwhelmed
when in small parts.

Not Here

the sky is red and my
dog bite scar tells me
rain is coming even
though clouds have yet
to grace the sky

a wind whispers lies
as it caresses past
with an autumn chill
despite the high summer
sun and the trees full
of purple leaves

far from home and the
grass isn’t greener
it’s not even green
and a too bright orange
raccoon scurries up
a tree.

a constant tune is in the
distance never closer
never farther just at
the level where I have to
question if I even hear the chords

it's peaceful but there are no
people or cities or sounds of

anything but nature
and maybe that's why its
calming

no obligations under the
purple leafed trees with
bark that matches the sky
no pressure other then
the automatic
in out in out in out
of breathing

some point I’ll find the
cabinet, closet, Tupperware back
I should find the exit
probably
maybe
but the distant music shifts
to lullaby and the wind’s lies
sound almost like truth
as my eyes close and I can
rest without the anxiety of society
I’ll get back later
there is usually a later
it’ll be fine
yes
fine

Greetings

It is time to toast with grape soda
from the floor as I practice the
antiquated chalk outlines of old
playing possum into the new year
to sneak past the bad luck
that has clung onto me for too long
as the artificial sparkle of grape
graces my tongue and I curse
time passing and stagnating
but going oh so fast too
as I plan out my angry cake
to gobble this year in
sweet chocolate and ugly frosting
as people shoot off illegal fireworks
another sip of lollipop grape soda
a lick of ice cream and
unvoiced promises I will keep
this time for sure
I tap the can against Houdini's head
To seal the deal as her soft snores
Fill the air
It is time to toast and keep promises

www.ingramcontent.com/pod-product-compliance
Lightning Source LLC
Chambersburg PA
CBHW051756130826
49812CB00033B/1179
9789357216807